Looking Closely
through the Forest

FRANK SERAFINI

Kids Can Press

Look very  closely.

What do you see?

Lizard tongues?
Flickering flames?
What could it be?

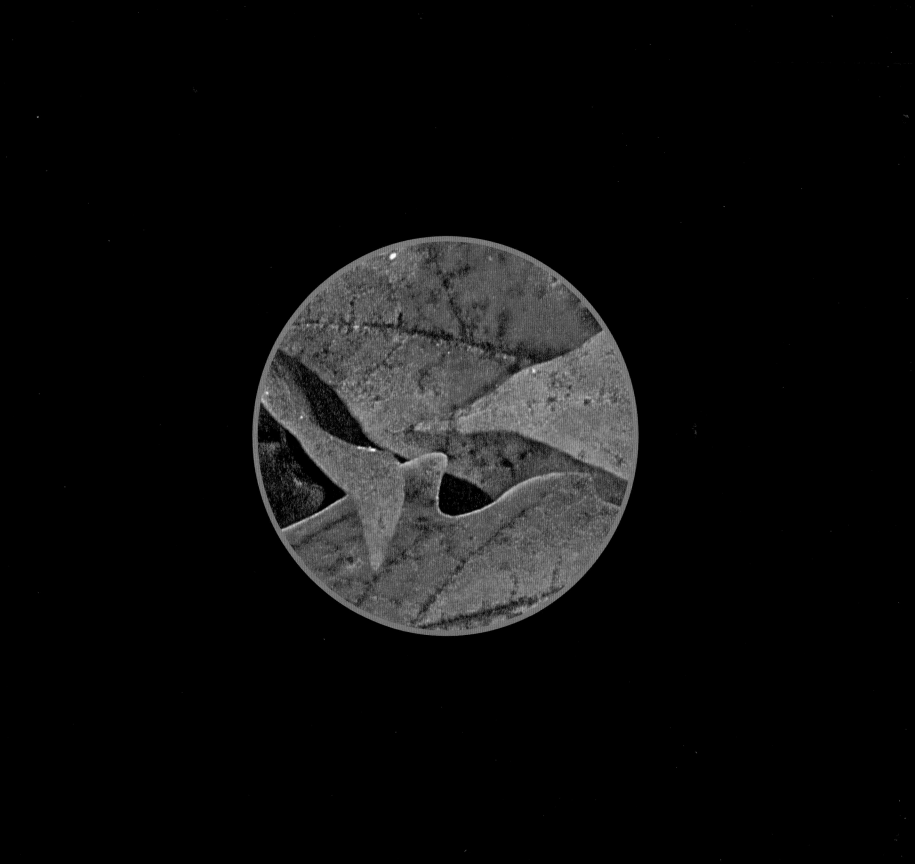

It's a *Sugar Maple* Leaf.

Every autumn you can find orange, red and yellow leaves scattered like a blanket across the forest floor. Most sugar maple leaves have five points. These bright red leaves can grow as large as an adult's hand. They fall from trees that can grow over 25 m (80 ft.) tall.

Sugar maples get their name from their sweet sap. People drill a hole in the tree trunk to collect the sap. Then they boil it to make maple syrup.

Look very closely.

What do you see?

A whirligig?
A butterfly wing?
What could it be?

It's a *Sego Lily.*

When you walk through the forest, look closely for flowers that bloom in the spring and summer. Some wildflowers grow in the shade of the forest. Others need more sunlight to bloom.

The sego lily blooms from May to July. The cup-shaped flower grows in sunny patches in grasslands and pine forests. Its colorful insides look like the patterns of a kaleidoscope.

Look very  closely.

What do you see?

Flakes of oatmeal?
A moldy orange?
What could it be?

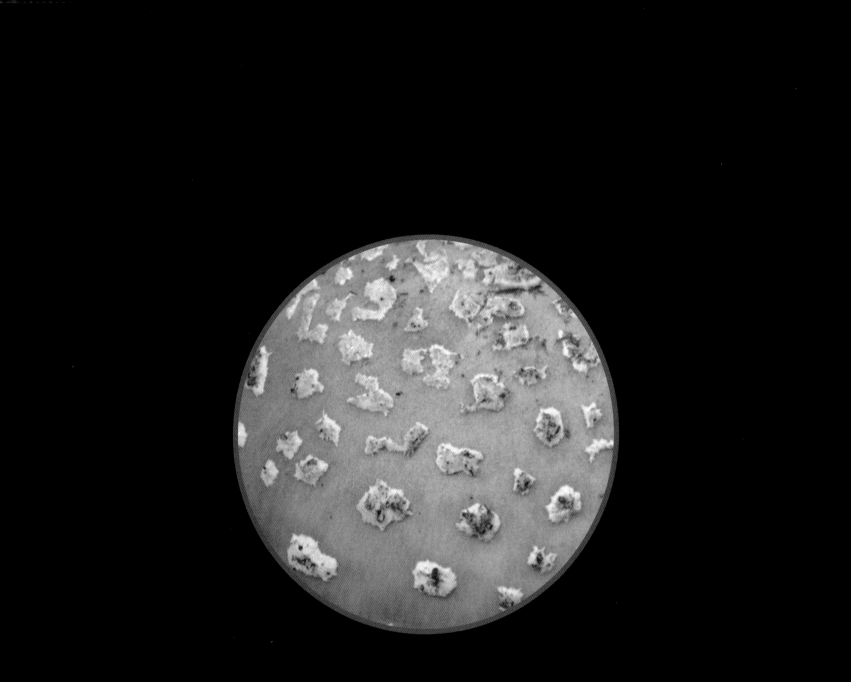

It's a Spotted Toadstool.

Toadstools are also called mushrooms. People harvest some types of mushrooms, but not all mushrooms are safe to eat or touch. It is better to simply look because many wild toadstools are poisonous.

Spotted toadstools get their name from the patterns on their caps. The small white spots are called warts.

Look very closely.

What do you see?

A cave in the snow?
A polar bear's nose?
What could it be?

It's an Aspen Tree.

Aspens are deciduous trees that grow in the Rocky Mountains. Deciduous trees lose their leaves in the winter. Aspens grow in groups. Each tree in the group shares roots underground.

Aspen bark is smooth and hard to peel. The dark, eye-shaped marks on aspen bark are called beards. Like scars, they show where a branch once fell from the tree's trunk.

Look very  closely.

What do you see?

Gummy candy?
A bicycle tire?
What could it be?

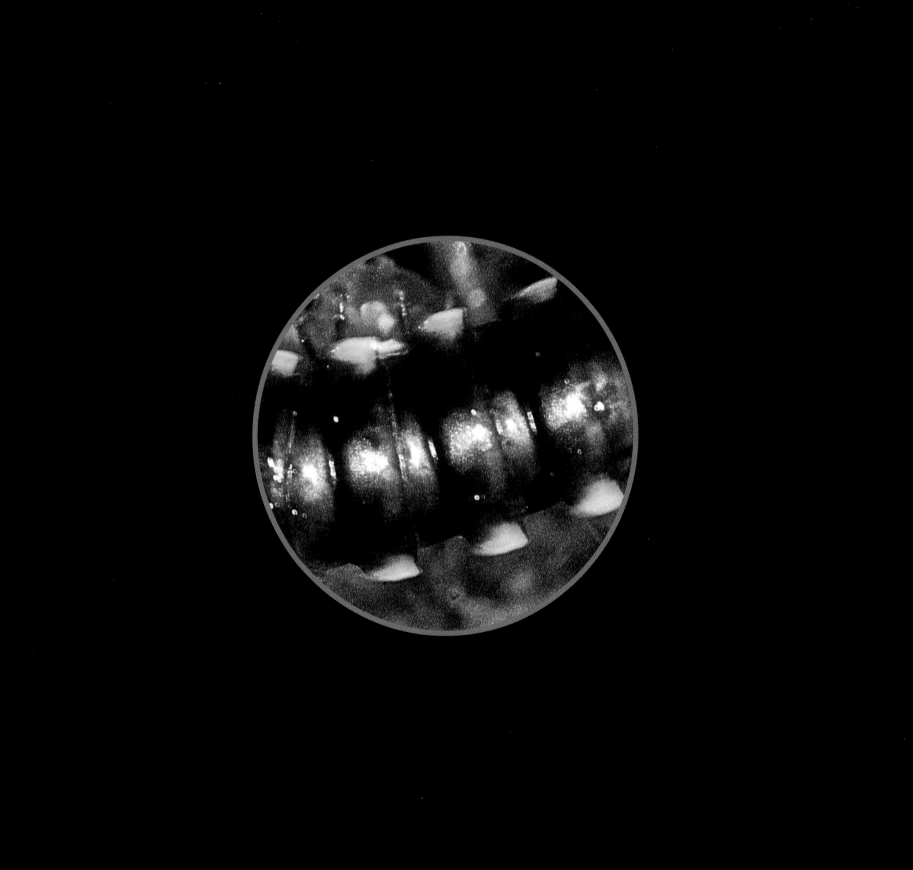

It's a Yellow-Spotted Millipede.

Millipede means "thousand feet," but yellow-spotted millipedes have only 62. They move their feet in pairs. Their legs ripple like waves when they walk.

The yellow-spotted millipede uses its antennae to feel its way along the forest floor. When it gets scared, it curls into a ball. Its hard shell protects it from predators. The yellow-spotted millipede can also frighten enemies with a poisonous smell. The smell can kill a beetle, but it will not hurt humans.

Look very closely.

What do you see?

A tree stump?
A moth wing?
What could it be?

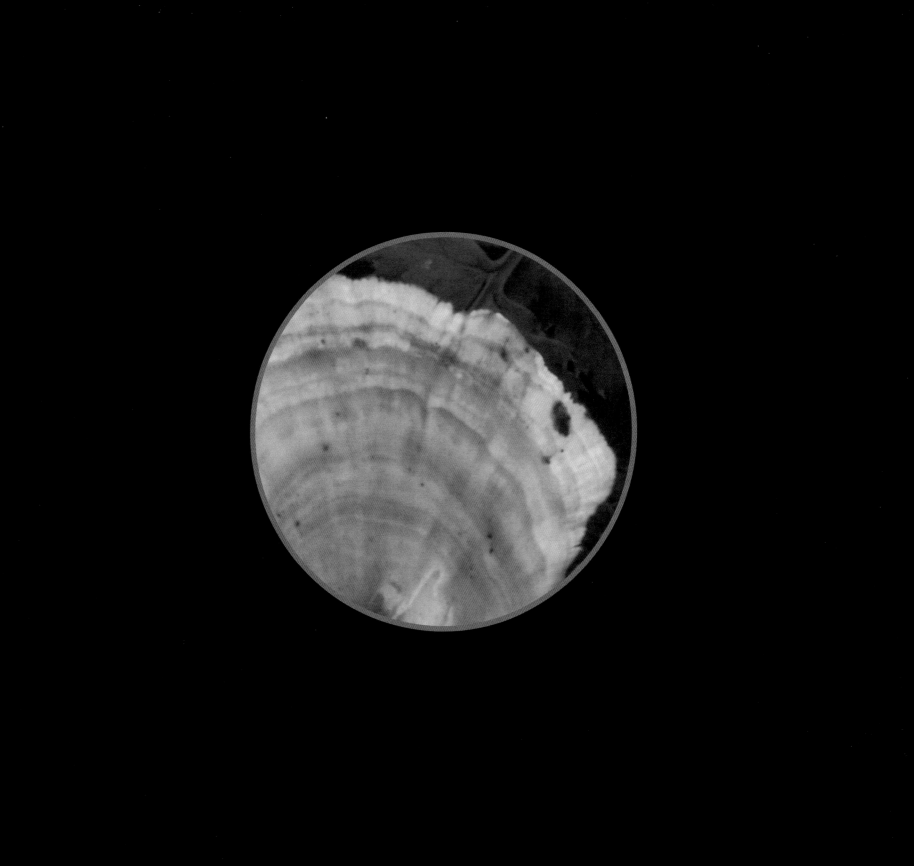

It's a Turkey Tail Fungus.

Fungi grow in all types of forests around the world. They are related to mushrooms and toadstools. Fungi feed on dead plants. They recycle nutrients into the soil for other plants and trees to use.

Turkey tail fungi grow like shelves on tree stumps and fallen logs. They have tough, leathery tops and soft, white bellies. They are called turkey tail fungi because the stripes on top look like a turkey's tail feathers.

Look very  closely.

What do you see?

A woolly scarf?
An insect leg?
What could it be?

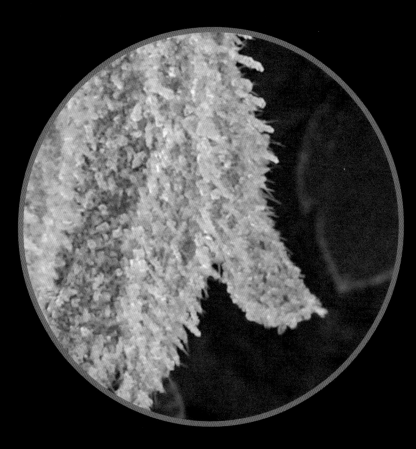

It's Frost on a Leaf.

Early in the morning, when the weather is damp and cold, look closely at the forest floor. You might see ice crystals, called frost, gathered along the tiny hairs of a leaf.

Frost forms on chilly mornings when moisture in the air cools very quickly. If the air is cold enough, the moisture will freeze onto grass, leaves and twigs. Ice crystals build on top of each other to make patterns like snowflakes. When the sun warms the air, frost melts away.

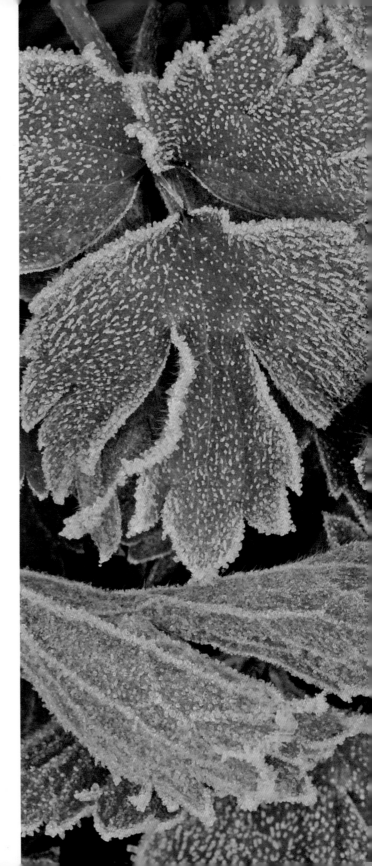

Look very closely.

What do you see?

Chocolate chips?
A pineapple?
What could it be?

It's a Pinecone.

Pinecones come in all shapes and sizes. Some of the biggest evergreen trees, like the mighty sequoia, can have the smallest pinecones.

Closed pinecones hang from tree branches. They look like they are covered in hard fish scales. The scales protect a tree's seeds until they are ready to grow. Open pinecones have already let their seeds go. Each seed has a "wing" that helps it float to the ground.

Look very closely.

What do you see?

A brass button?
A dragon's eye?
What could it be?

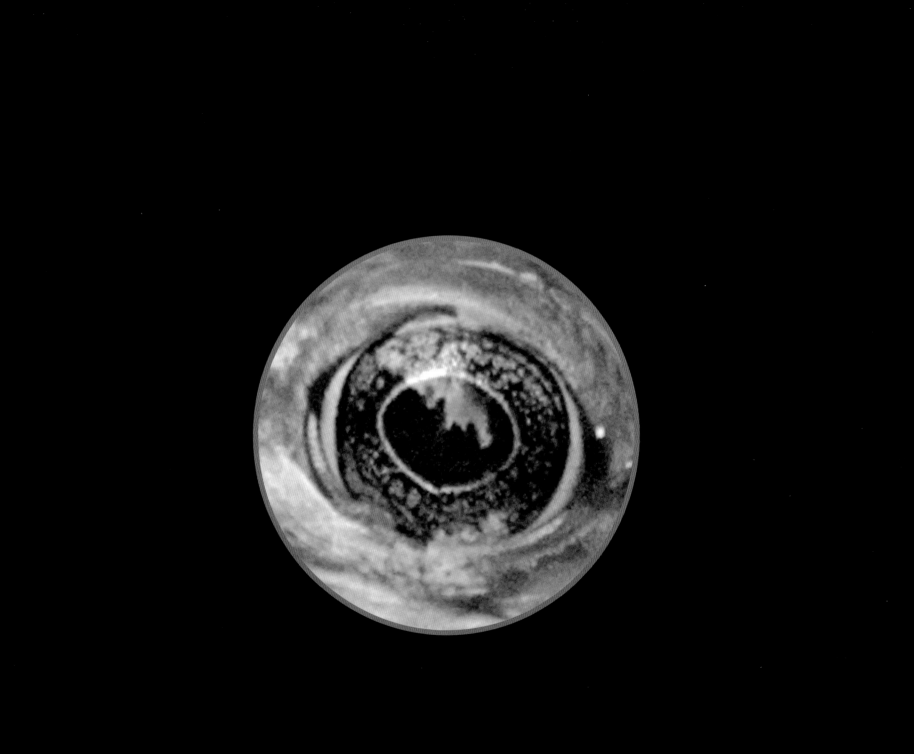

It's a
Green Frog.

Frogs live near ponds, lakes and streams in the forest. They can be hard to find because they sit very still when hunting. Frogs flip out their long, sticky tongues to grab flies, spiders and even snails.

Although they are called green frogs, they can be brown, green or even blue! Green frogs use their color to hide from birds, snakes and raccoons. Their large eyes bulge out so that they can see in many directions.

**To my friend David Middleton, photographer extraordinaire.
Thank you for helping me point my camera in new directions.**

Photographer's Note

Photographers pay attention to things that most people overlook or take for granted. I can spend hours wandering along the shore, through the forest, across the desert or in my garden, looking for interesting things to photograph. My destination is not a place, but rather a new way of seeing.

It takes time to notice things. To be a photographer, you have to slow down and imagine in your "mind's eye" what the camera can capture. Ansel Adams said you could discover a whole life's worth of images in a six-square-foot patch of Earth. In order to do so, you have to look very closely.

By creating the images featured in this series of picture books, I hope to help people attend to nature, to things they might have normally passed by. I want people to pay attention to the world around them, to appreciate what nature has to offer, and to begin to protect the fragile environment in which we live.

Text and photographs © 2008 Frank Serafini

Pages 38–39: San Juan Mountains, United States of America Back cover: Queensland, Australia

Kids Can Press acknowledges the financial support of the Government of Ontario, through the Ontario Media Development Corporation's Ontario Book Initiative.

Published in Canada by	Published in the U.S. by
Kids Can Press Ltd.	Kids Can Press Ltd.
25 Dockside Drive	2250 Military Road
Toronto, ON M5A 0B5	Tonawanda, NY 14150

www.kidscanpress.com

Edited by Karen Li
Designed by Julia Naimska

This book is smyth sewn casebound.
Manufactured in Tseung Kwan O, Kowloon, Hong Kong, China, in 11/2010 by Paramount Printing Co. Ltd.

CM 08 0 9 8 7 6 5 4 3 2

Library and Archives Canada Cataloguing in Publication

Serafini, Frank
Looking closely through the forest / Frank Serafini.

(Looking closely)
ISBN 978-1-55453-212-4

1. Forest plants—Juvenile literature. 2. Forest animals—Juvenile literature. I. Title. II. Title: Through the forest. III. Series: Looking closely (Toronto, Ont.)

QH86.S44 2008   j578.73   C2007-902575-7

Kids Can Press is a *corus*™ Entertainment company